The Book on
The Art of Dancing

THE BOOK ON
The Art of Dancing

ANTONIO CORNAZANO

TRANSLATED BY

MADELEINE INGLEHEARN

AND

PEGGY FORSYTH

INTRODUCTION AND NOTES BY

MADELEINE INGLEHEARN

NOVERRE PRESS

First published in 1981 by Dance Books Ltd

This facsimile reprint published in 2011 by
The Noverre Press
Southwold House
Isington Road
Binsted
Hampshire
GU34 4PH

© 2011 Madeleine Inglehearn

ISBN 978-1-906830-38-0

A CIP catalogue record for this book is available from the British Library

Contents

INTRODUCTION 9

THE BOOK ON
THE ART OF DANCING 16

NOTES 37

MUSIC 46

Introduction

Two of the best known works of the Italian Renaissance are Baldassar Castiglione's *Il Libro del Cortegiano*[1] (The Book of the Courtier), written by him in 1508 though not published until 1528, and Nicolo Machiavelli's *Il Principe*[2] (The Prince) published in 1513. Both set out to instruct Italian princes in the qualities necessary to succeed in life. Machiavelli was concerned mainly with material success and temporal power:

> A Prince cannot observe all those things for which men are held good; he being often forc'd, for the maintenance of his State, to do contrary to his faith, charity, humanity and religion: and therefore it behooves him to have a mind so dispos'd as to turne and take the advantage of all winds and fortunes; and as formerly I said, not forsake the good while he can; but to know how to make use of the evill upon necessity.

Castiglione aims to define the fully rounded character of a 'Courtier' in which wisdom, statesmanship and learning are combined with social graces and wit. Castiglione's courtier must be well read, a master of languages and able to talk pleasantly and intelligently on all subjects but without any sign of boasting. He must be a brave and chivalrous soldier though not too quick to seek a fight. He should be a competent athlete and sportsman, have a certain skill in music and be an excellent horseman and dancer.

Castiglione's book is based on a gathering in March 1507 at the Court of the Duke of Urbino, where the Duchess Elizabetta Gonzaga and her close friend Lady Emilia Pia presided over the entertainments of the evening. In Castiglione's words:

> ... the maner of the gentlemen in the house was immediately after supper to assemble together where the Dutchesse was. Where among other recreations, musicke and dauncing, which they used continually, sometime they propounded feate questions.

One such 'feate question'—what makes the perfect Courtier—is the subject of Castiglione's book, and it paints a fascinating picture of the Renaissance ideal of manhood.

As we have seen, one of the skills essential to a good Courtier was dancing, though Castiglione has certain reservations:

> There be some other exercises that may be done both openly and privately as dancing: and in this I believe the Courtier ought to have respect, for if he daunceth in the presence of many and in a place full of people, he must (in my minde) keepe a certain dignitie, tempered nothwithstanding, with a handsome and sightly sweetnesse of gestures.

He also defines the accomplishments and graces necessary for a gentlewoman:

> I will that this woman have a sight in letters, in musicke, in drawing or painting, and skilfull in dauncing, and in devising sports and pastimes.

though he warns:

> ... when she cometh to daunce, or to shew any kinde of musicke, she ought to be brought to it with suffring herselfe somewhat to be prayed, and with a certain bashfulnesse.

There had been many books of etiquette written before Castiglione, aimed at educating and instructing the young. *The Book of the Knight of La Tour-Landry* and Jacques Le Grand's *Boke of good maners*, both translated by William Caxton in the fourteenth century, and the thirteenth-century treatise of Walter de Biblesworth,[3] all set a high moral and intellectual standard, but only in Italy was equal emphasis placed on artistic skills and accomplishments. The Italian courts vied with each other to attract the finest musicians, painters and poets, and great families like the d'Estes of Ferrara, the Sforzas in Milan, or the Gonzagas at Mantua gave their patronage to artists from all over Europe. From the middle of the fifteenth century we also find dancing masters taking an important place in the artistic life of the courts. We have a note of Duchess Bona of Milan sending her dancing master to the Court of the d'Estes to teach the two young princesses Isabella and Beatrice,[4] while the young Hyppolita Sforza took her dancing master with her when she went to Naples as the bride of Alfonso Duke of Calabria.

The greatest dancing master of this period seems to have been one Messer Domenico of Piacenza, also known as Domenico of Ferrara, whom all the others acknowledge as their master and peer. Of his pupils, three are known to us today through their writings. They were Guglielmo Ebreo, Johannis Ambrosio and Antonio Cornazano. Cornazano's treatise on dance is dated 1455, while one of Guglielmo's works is dated 1463. It appears there-therefore that Domenico himself must have been working and teaching during the period 1430/50, while his pupils continued to spread his ideas on dance throughout the second half of the fifteenth century. Indeed, some of the dances survived well into the sixteenth century and three (*Rosinna*, *Anello* and *Gioiosa*) are named in the letters of Andrea Calmo, a minor poet who died in 1571. Calmo also refers to two of the major dance forms, *Saltarello* and *Bassadanza*.[5] Three dances (*Rosinna*, *Anello* and *Giove*) are also mentioned in an anonymous song text published in a collection of songs for three voices.[6] Each song in this collection represents a different profession and this one is sung by three dancing masters.

Otto Kinkeldey in his book *A Jewish Dancing Master of the Renaissance* has given us a detailed study of Guglielmo Ebreo.[7] There are in fact five works by Guglielmo all dealing with dance instruction and describing various dances, though some books contain many more dances than others. The copy in the Communal Library of Sienna contains a total of 60, while that at Modena has only 14. Unfortunately little is known about Guglielmo's background, although, as one of his treatises contains a dance composed by Lorenzo di Piero di Cosimo de Medici, it seems possible that he spent some part of his life at the Court of the Medici in Florence.

In the Bibliothèque Nationale in Paris, there is a treatise by Johannis Ambrosio which is almost identical with one of Guglielmo's works, and this led Kinkeldey to suggest that they were one and the same man. There may possibly have been a period when Guglielmo found it best not to publicise his race. It is interesting to find that in 1481 when the Marquis of Mantua sent his envoys to Ferrara to arrange a marriage between the Marquis's son and the seven-year-old Isabella d'Este, one of the company reported that he had watched Isabella dancing with her master Messer Ambrogio, a Jew.[8] Could this have been Guglielmo alias Johannis Ambrosio? Kindeldey quotes the existence of a letter signed 'Ambrogio Giovanni' sent from Naples to the mother of Hyppolita praising her daughter's skill in dancing and describing how she had delighted her audience by inventing two new *balli* to two French songs which she danced to her own singing. Again one wonders whether this Ambrogio was the same man that danced with the young Isabella d'Este some years later?

As for Antonio Cornazano, he is best known as a poet of considerable renown, and whether he was also a dancing master or simply an enthusiastic amateur of the art of dancing is not certain. His work is close in style to the treatise thought to have been written by Domenico himself and many of the dances described by Guglielmo and Ambrosio are dismissed by him as 'too old or too well known' to be worth setting down on paper. In a close comparison between Cornazano's work and that of Domenico, it becomes apparent that his boast that 'having heard it (a new dance) described or seen it danced only once, that was sufficient for me to join into the dance *dicto facto* and without further ado perform the same without a single error of judgement' was probably somewhat exaggerated. In several instances his steps fit awkwardly with his music, and both differ slightly from Domenico's version of the same dance in which the steps and music usually mould together so naturally and with such ease as to suggest the hand of a practised and gifted master. Cornazano's treatise is dedicated and addressed to Hyppolita Sforza and dated 1455, when Hyppolita was nine years old. A second copy of this same work was made some years later with the addition of a dedicatory poem to Sforza Secondo, Hyppolita's brother Galeazzo Maria who became the second Sforza Duke of Milan in 1466. It would seem from the use of the term Sforza Secondo that this second copy was written sometime after 1466, in other words, Hyppolita having married and left Milan, Cornazano presented his work to a new patron, but rather than rewrite it he left it with the original dedication and wording and simply tacked a new dedication on the beginning.

Francesco Sforza, Duke of Milan, was reputed to be a man of great charm with a warm personality which endeared his subjects to him in spite of the occasional display of ruthlessness and cunning. His wife Bianca Maria Visconti was an intellectual woman who took a close interest in the education of her children, employing the best possible teachers for them and supervising their studies personally. As a result the children became renowned for their learning. In 1459 when Pope Pius II came to the Congress of Mantua, the 13-year-old Hyppolita astonished the assembled prelates by delivering a long speech of welcome to the Pope in Latin. The Duchess also saw to it that her daughter mastered the art of dancing.

In 1465 Hyppolita, who had been married as a child to Alfonso Duke of Calabria set off on her journey to Naples and her new home. On the way she passed through Sienna where she was entertained by 12 dancers in 'una moresca'. After this we have only one small glimpse of her, charming her father-in-law and her new husband with her graceful dancing and singing.

Like many Renaissance princesses, Hyppolita was married for political expediency, and in spite of her father's geniality and her mother's loving care, she was married into one of the most vicious and depraved Courts of Europe. Her father-in-law Ferrante, King of Naples, was notorious for his cruelty, while of her husband Alfonso, a Flemish diplomat in the service of Charles VIII of France, wrote:

> Never was any prince more bloody, wicked, inhuman, lascivious or gluttonous than he.[9]

So this intelligent and artistic young woman, used to the comparatively happy atmosphere of her father's court in Milan, was thrown into the corrupt and violent society of Naples, and we have little further knowledge of her. She had two children. Her daughter Isabella married Hyppolita's nephew, son of Sforza Secondo, while her son Ferrantino succeeded his father to the throne of Naples in 1485, when Alfonso abdicated in terror and escaped to Sicily, leaving his son to fight the French invaders with courage but little success. Hyppolita, however, never saw this collapse of the House of Aragon for she had died the previous year at the age of 38.

In Cornazano's work we catch a glimpse of the education of a Renaissance princess. Her dancing was to develop in her, not only grace of movement and sweetness of demeanour (*Aere*), but a deeper understanding of musical rhythm (*Misura*), an appreciation of artistic shapes and patterns (*Compartimento di terreno*) the subtle beauty of variety in form and movement (*Diversita di cose*), and above all a good memory. With such accomplishments she would hope to become the 'Queen of Feasts' and rule the hearts of her subjects.

COMINCIA LIBRO DELL'ARTE DEL DANZARE INTITULATO E COMPOSTO PER ANTONIO CORNAZANO ALLA ILLUSTRE MADONNA HIPPOLYTA DUCHESSA DI CALABRIA. 1455.

Amazonica nympha, Inclyta diva
di leda figlia non ma di diana
nel cui materno exempio honesta e piana
infinita belleza aggionge a riva

Giusto amor m'ha constrecto ch'io vi scriva
che l'arte gia insegnata non sia vana
poi che compresi quanta altiera humana
in si giovinil cor virtu fioriva

La piu matura eta che'n voi s'expecta
col studio di questa opra chio vi noto
vi fara dea fra l'altre donne electa

Intenderete q'il legiadro moto
de piedi in ballo et se'l mio dir s'accetta
in quanto io vaglio a voi tutto m'avoto.

HERE BEGINS THE BOOK ON THE ART OF DANCING DEDICATED AND WRITTEN BY ANTONIO CORNAZANO TO THE ILLUSTRIOUS LADY HYPPOLITA DUCHESS OF CALABRIA. 1455.

Nymph from the Amazon, excellent goddess, daughter not of Leda but of Diana, in whose Mother's image, honest and clear, infinite beauty is proclaimed to the farthest shore.

Love has rightly ordained that I should set down in writing the art which I have taught so that it may not be lost, for I have come to see the flowering of a gentle and human virtue in so young a heart.

The increasing maturity to which we look forward, and the perusal of this work which I write for you, will make you a goddess amongst chosen women.

Here you will learn the delights of dancing feet: and if my work is accepted whatever my worth, I dedicate myself wholeheartedly to you.

Memoria (Memory)

Perfection in dancing is *Misura* (Measure), *Maniera* (Manner), *Aere* (Spirit), *Diversita di cose* (Variety), *Compartimento di terreno* (Use of space).

You must have Memory so as to remember the steps you are about to perform when you begin to dance. You must have Measure so that as well as remembering the dance you may move measuredly and in agreement with your musician. While remembering the dance and moving measuredly Manner lies in the grace of the movements you make, balancing and undulating with the body according to the foot that moves, so that if you move the right foot to make a double you must balance on the left foot which remains firm on the ground, turning the body somewhat towards that side and undulating in the second short step raising yourself smoothly and then very gently lowering yourself on the third which makes the double. Spirit in dancing is that especial grace which you must have above all others and which will make you pleasing to the eyes of those who are watching; and above all everything must be done with a joyousness and gaiety of countenance. Variety lies in the art of knowing how to dance the dances differently and not forever repeating the same steps, so that you have *sempi, dopii, riprese, continente, volte tonde* and *mezo volte* in various guises, and what is done once must not be immediately repeated a second time: but this last point applies more particularly to the man than to the lady. Use of space is understanding how to take into account the appointed area in which you are about to dance, diligently calculating the space and steps which you will perform there, being master in the art of using space, and above all else this must be carried out with a joyousness of spirit.

May I say that if these aspects are observed, there is no lady so ugly that she may not appear beautiful, or man so small that he may not appear large, and each of them skilful and graceful.

And as a living example may I say that if Your Grace imitates that queen of feasts, the Illustrious Lady Beatrice, you cannot go wrong, and so as to illustrate her legendary graces may I digress and tell you of a proverb from Ferrara:

> He who wishes to enter another world, let him listen to the music of Piero Bono.
> He who wishes to see the Heavens open, let him experience the beneficence of Duke Borso.
> He who wishes to have heaven on earth, let him look upon My Lady Beatrice presiding over a feast.

Dancing consists of four principal measures. *Piva, Saltarello, Quaternaria* and *Bassadanza*. The *Piva* is nothing other than double steps executed at an accelerated pace because of the fastness of the measure which incites the dancer to it. The *Saltarello* is the gayest of all the dances, the Spanish calling it the *alta danza*. It simply consists of doubles which are undulated because of the rising movement of the second short step that beats in the middle of one tempo and the next, balanced by the movement of the first step which carries the body forward as I have explained. The *Quaternaria* is really called the german *saltarello* and it consists of two simples with a little *ripresa* executed after the second sideways step. The *Bassadanza* is queen of the other measures and has to be accompanied by all the other properties given in the above definition of the dance.

The *Piva* was the principal and foundation of all the other measures, from which the others are evolved and linked together, so that from the *Piva* we get the *bassadanza* and from the *bassadanza* the *piva*. From the *saltarello* we get a condensed *bassadanza* as you will see in the plan which I will show you. From the *quaternaria* we get the natural *bassadanza* and the *saltarello* and *piva*, so that considering the matter well, each measure evolves from the *piva* because it derives from it, almost as the flow of a river with its many tributaries.

Although with our forebears the *piva* was the principal sound used in dancing, nowadays intellects have developed and flowered into greater refinement and amongst the nobility and good dancers it has been discarded and has fallen from use.

However, should it happen to be danced, it is not right for the lady to do other than its own natural steps, assisting the man during the turns according to the exchanges and jumps he has to do, forward and back and in and out, and she must be quick and well practised in this because of the measure which is faster than all the others.

In the *saltarello*, apart from its own natural steps, balanced and undulated in the manner described above, it is lovely if the lady intersperses some things with sweetness of manner, such as two simples balanced and undulated in a single beat and sometimes three *contrapassi* in two beats, and one can do these things one after the other, or on their own should one wish: but in this case the lady should never detach her tempo from the ground, nor should the man, or extremely rarely if he is a good dancer.

The measure of the *quaternaria* is not much used on its own by the Italians in dancing, but sometimes, interspersed with other dances it may be used to ornament them, as for instance in the fifth part of the SOBRIA where the men change places and come up behind the lady; and as in the sixth part of the PREGIONERA where the man takes the lady.

In the *bassadanza*, apart from the steps of which it is composed, and the balancing and undulating movements of the body, it is not beautiful unless one makes the *riprese* and the *continenze* differ from one another, that is large and small. After a large step one should never follow on with another; and vice versa. Sometimes to hold a tempo and leave it in suspense is not considered to be ugly, but you must then enter into the sequence with a lightness of manner, almost as if the body were brought back from death into life. On this point, your good servant and my master Misser Domenichino, showed irrefutable judgment when he said that dancing, particularly in the slow measure, must continue to appear as an illusive shadow, in which image many things can be expressed which cannot otherwise be put into words.

Let those masters of frivolities and charlatans hold their tongues therefore, for this is the only refined manner in which to dance; and to remove this from the *bassadanza* is to transform it into coarse movements so that it loses all its natural qualities.

Dancing contains within itself nine movements, natural and material, and three accidentals. The naturals are: simples, doubles, *riprese, continente contrapassi, movimenti, volte tonde, meza volte,* and *scambii.* The accidentals are, *trascorse, frappamenti,* and *pizigamenti*; and none of these accidentals is right performed on their own, though the *pizigamento* is less becoming than the others. Of all the naturals in the *piva* none is performed save one, and this is the double which is very fast because of the condensed measure. In the *saltarello* one does four naturals, simples and *riprese* in the *bassadanza,* and doubles and *contrapassi* all within their length; and he who makes the *contrapassi* will put in three in the time of two doubles; and these doubles in *saltarello* are not as fast as those of the *piva* because the measure has been broadened by as much as can be seen in the chart which I have made below. In the *saltarello todescho*, that is, in the *quaternaria* because it contains the other measures according to the one which is being danced, only the appropriate movements will be brought to it, so that when dancing in *piva* you will only perform the steps pertaining to *piva*; and so with the other measures derived from it. The *bassadanza* can contain all nine naturals, except the *movimento*, which is not used apart from the *balliti*, and this is not a perfect tempo, but is used in public by the men in answer to the ladies' *movimento* as in LEONCELLO and many other dances, and all of these are lovely for the lady in whatever measure she should dance them, provided she balances and undulates her body in the described manner.

I shall not further define the accidental movements, as they in no way embellish the dancing of the lady: it is enough to have specified what they are called, so that by virtue of their vocabulary they are intelligible enough to all dancers.

The *balliti* are a composition of several measures in which all the natural material movements can be contained, each with its own fundamental characteristic, as for instance in the MERCANTIA and in the SOBRIA, which are completely contrary to each other, so that in one the lady gives audience to all and sundry, were there a thousand present, and in the other she looks to no one except he with whom she was first partnered; and it is particularly necessary in these last dances to have a good memory. I offer myself, Your Grace, as an example so as to demonstrate an infallible rule; something which I do not believe can be shown by any living dancer, and it is this; not only can I remember the themes of dances once studied, but often when I was in the most refined assembly rooms, I mean during the flower and ardour of my youth, and being unexpectedly confronted with a new *ballo* or *bassadanza*, having heard it described or seen it danced only once, that was sufficient for me to join into the *ballo dicto fatto* and without further ado perform the same without a single error of judgment etc.

        Two simple *passi* equal one tempo
        One double is one tempo
        One *ripresa* i. tempo
        Two *continente* i. tempo
        Three *contrapassi* ii. tempo
        Volta tonda ii. tempo
        Meza volta i. tempo
        The *scambii* either i. tempo or none
        In the *movimenti* there is no rule
        The accidentals are as you will.

Again in dancing one does not only observe the measure of the music, but a measure which is other than musical, on the contrary it is outside these things, and it is the measuring of the lightness within the undulating movement of rising, so that one is always rising the one way; because otherwise the measure would be broken.

Undulating is simply a slow rising of the whole body followed by the sudden lowering of it.

Apart from the *balliti*; the dances which are most often performed by us Italians in noble assembly rooms are the *saltarello* and the *bassadanza*. The *saltarello* as I have said, is called the *altadanza* by the Spanish, and it is the *pas de brebant*, attendant (the servant) to the *bassadanza* which is always danced after it.

In the *bassadanza* every tempo is divided into four parts. The void is one part, which is the first rising movement, each of the three following steps take up a quarter which completes the four: that which is the void and that which is the remaining three-quarters is difficult to explain without being present to demonstrate it.

Now, so as to give Your Grace more palpable evidence of all the measures, I will, by means of a ladder demonstrate the steps up which those who wish to excel must climb; and contrary to all the others which are wide at the bottom and narrow at the top, this one is narrow at the bottom and wide above, so that he who wishes to ascend it requires the greatest dexterity if he is not to let the ladder waver under his feet. Here is the plan.

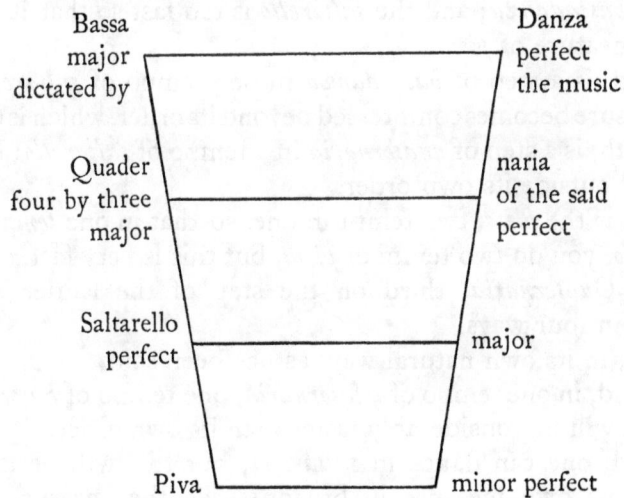

The *Piva* is the first step of this ladder, and it is smaller than all the others by as much as can be seen here with one's own eyes: it is a country dance from which all the others are developed and it is the sound of the reed pipes found amongst the shepherds. From the oat reeds the music passed into the marsh reeds. From that, with the refinement of intellects, the music passed into the flutes and the other instruments made and played by ourselves today, and filled with such music as gives us no need to envy heaven itself. And so it developed, and it can be danced in four ways, the four variations being shown here.

The first way is its own natural way.

The second is an extension of the natural way, which is to dance the *piva* with the steps of the *saltarello* shown on the second step of the ladder; so that in every two *tempi* of *piva* one does one step of *saltarello*, but as that is too slow the *saltarello* is extended beyond its own natural *tempo* by a third, as I have said, and is outside its natural *tempo*.

Third, is two *tempi* of *piva* for one step of *bassadanza*.

Fourth, is one step of *quaternaria* over two *tempi* of *piva*; but this is slow and is outside its order by a sixth or thereabouts.

Saltarello, second step on the said ladder, can be danced in five ways.

First its own natural way.

Second in *bassadanza*, imposing two steps of *saltarello* for one step of *bassadanza*; and the *saltarello* is too fast so that it returns to the measure of *piva*.

Third, is a step of *bassadanza* in one tempo of *saltarello*; but the measure becomes compressed beyond its order, which is too fast.

Fourth, is a step of *quaternaria* in a tempo of *saltarello*; but it is fast and outside its own order.

Fifth is the *piva*, two tempi in one, so that in one *tempo* of the *saltarello*, you do two tempi of *piva*, but this is very fast.

The *Quaternaria*, third on the step of the ladder, can be danced in four ways.

First, in its own natural way, as has been said.

Second, in one tempo of *quaternaria*, one tempo of *bassadanza*; but this will be considerably faster than its own order.

Third, one can dance in *saltarello*; but this will be as much outside its own measure in broadness as the measure of the *bassadanza* is constricted outside its own.

Fourth, two tempi of *piva* for one tempo of *quaternaria*; and the *piva* will then be considerably faster than its own measure.

The *Bassadanza*, fourth on the step of the said ladder, one can dance in five ways.

First, its own natural way.

Second, in *piva*, two in one measure of *bassadanza*, both these have their own order.

Third, in the *quaternaria* step, which will be a little slow.

Fourth, in *saltarello*, by doing one step of *saltarello* to one tempo of *bassadanza*; but this will be too slow.

Fifth, still in *saltarello*, by doing two steps of *saltarello* to one tempo of *bassadanza*, but this will be so fast that the steps will be like those of the *piva*.

All the measures may be alternated, and one can impose one upon the other in the said fashion, and this is an art requiring a perfection of skill not always possessed by scholars. The diagram of the said ladder will demonstrate the various ways in which the measures can be altered, and by how much they can be broadened or accelerated.

The given rules are sufficient to achieve perfection in the use of measures, without which skill, nothing is achieved.

Now we come to those *balli* and *bassedanze* outside the ordinary and which have been composed for noble halls, and to be danced only by the greatest ladies, and not by the populace.
To begin
MERCANTIA is a dance which is appropriately named. One lady only dances with three men, and she gives audience to all, however many were present, and as though she were a merchant of lovers—and it begins like this—The lady's hand is held by the man in front, two other men are behind them both hand in hand.

In this order they dance eleven tempi of *saltarello*, and then stop. Afterwards the men who are behind the lady spread out from each other with six diagonal *riprese*, one to the left, and the other to the right. Then the lady does a *meza volta* turning to the left, and the man who is her partner goes forward with three doubles, beginning on the left foot. The man who is now at the lady's right hand sets off with two simples and a double, beginning with the left; and goes to touch the hand of the lady, and without taking any time he turns to the right hand with two simples and a double, beginning with the right foot, and returning to the place where he was before. Afterwards his partner, who is on the left hand, does the same; and the lady, each time that one of these two has touched her hand, does a *volta tonda*, while he is returning to his own place. Then the man who is in front, as though he were being called, does a *meza volta* to the right. Then the two men who are behind take each other by the hand and go forward with two simples and a double beginning with the right foot and they change places with each other. Afterwards the man who is in front sets off with two tempi of *saltarello*, starting with the left foot, and goes beside the lady. As though she were being called, the lady immediately turns towards the man, and the man touches her hand making a reverence on the left foot, and two *continenze* beginning with the left foot. Afterwards that same man goes to the left-hand side of the lady and with two simples and a double goes to take the place of the man who is behind on the right-hand side; and he who was on the left-hand side comes to fetch the lady with those steps, and he remains with the lady so that each in his turn dances with her: and so begin again.

To begin

JOVE is a dance that is danced in three: with the lady in the middle and the two men in single file, one in front and the other behind. In this order, together they dance three tempi of the *saltarello todescho* and a *volta tonda* in *bassadanza*; this is done twice; then the man who is in front turns around and faces the lady and she faces him, they then touch hands with a double to the right and then the lady stops, the companion who is behind comes up to meet the one who has just left the lady, with a double on the left foot: and the one who has left the lady goes towards his companion and that companion then goes to his place touching the hand of the lady and she goes to his place with a double on the right foot, and turning round to where she was first without taking any time. Then together they do two simples on the left (tired) foot and one double. Then together they repeat the steps which they first did when they changed places with each other in coming to touch the hand of the lady. Then everyone immediately does nine doubles together on one foot, that is the left (tired) foot, each one turning around as they reach the front so that at the end of the nine doubles the lady remains in the middle. Then all together they do two tempi of the *saltarello* and the lady stops, the men do a further two steps, one into the place of the other: then the lady does a *volta tonda* in *bassadanza*; this *saltarello* is done twice, changing places as before, and the lady does another *volta tonda* in *bassadanza*, and touching hands the man in front turns around to face the lady, and then he who is behind—and so begin again.

To begin

VERZEPPE is a dance almost similar to a skirmish: it is done by five, two ladies and three men in a line; the ladies in the middle. In this order they do a *saltarello* all together and then stop. Then the man in the middle and the man at the end set off and circle round the ladies with two doubles starting on the left foot, and then two doubles on the one foot, and go back to their places. The ladies make a *volta tonda* and the same steps the men have just done. The men do a *volta tonda*, then they all move forward together with three *contrapassi* beginning with the left foot, and turning around on the third (*contrapassi*), they come back with the same steps, and they turn around again and then stop. Then the man in front does a *meza volta* in the time of one tempo and goes to the place of the man at the back in *saltarello*, weaving through the ladies, and in this manner the man at the back comes to the place of the man in front leaving at the same time, and weaving through the ladies in the opposite way so that they do not collide. The ladies then set off with three doubles, to change places one with the other, the lady in front moving to the right-hand side on the left foot, and the lady behind moving to the left-hand side starting on the left foot: then the man in front and the man behind circle round them in *saltarello* and return to their places. Then the ladies return to their original place, as described above. Then the man in the middle, taking up a tempo, circles round the lady in front in *saltarello* and returns to his place. Then the men do a *movimento* which the ladies answer, and the men do a *volta tonda*. Then the ladies do a *movimento* which the men answer, and the ladies do that same *volta* (*tonda*) and so end.

But remember that this *volta* begins with the left foot because the measure is not that of the *bassadanza*.

BEREGUARDO NOVA is a dance that is danced by three, that is two men with the lady in the middle and the men on each side. In this order they all do a *saltarello* together and then stop. Then the man who is leading the lady does four doubles forward, without her, starting on the left foot, and the man below does two doubles towards the back and as he finishes these two he turns around and does the other two towards the lady who is in front of him in line, and behind the man who first set off. After completing the four doubles they all do three *contrapassi* together on the right foot and turn around to the right with two *continentie*, then with those same steps they go back to the place they came from, and in the same manner they turn round all together with two *continentie* and a *reverentia* on the left foot.

They then take a tempo of *saltarello* all together and the lady stops as she did the first time, and the man in front repeats the same steps that he first did, and returns to the lady coming back on the right foot and the man behind repeats both the movements as before, and together they come to take the lady in the middle; and immediately, as she is taken in the middle, the lady moves forward with a double on the right foot, and the men go after her with the same movement.

Then, all together they do a tempo of *saltarello*, at the end of which movement the lady stops, and the man who is on the left-hand side of the lady changes place with his companion, with a further tempo of *saltarello* going in front of the lady: and the man on the right-hand side goes to his place with the same step passing behind the lady. Then they do two *continenze* all together, and two doubles all together, at the end of which the lady stops, and the man on her left does a double forward, and the man on her right hand does it towards the back, both of them beginning with the left foot, and turning around at the end of the same tempo, they go back to their places with the right foot: and he who went forward with a double turns round on the right foot when he comes to the lady, and then all together they do three *continenze* and a *reverenza* on the left foot: and so begin again.

LEONCELLO NOVO is a dance that is done in three, two men and the lady in the middle side by side. In this order they all do three *contrapassi* beginning on the left foot. Then the lady goes forward with a double on the right foot, and the men go after her with the same step. Then the lady goes forward again with another double, and the men follow her. Then the lady sets off with her left foot to the left-hand side, and circles round the two men in *piva* and goes back to her place. Then the men set off in *saltarello* of *quaternaria* and do three tempi, and on the third tempo they turn right around taking the beat with their left foot and they turn their backs to the lady. The lady responds with the same steps; but she does not do the full turn only a *meza volta* in the last tempo and turns her back on the men: then all at once they set off in their opposite directions, the lady above and the men below with three *contrapassi* on the left, and they come towards each other with three *contrapassi* on the right and then turn back to back, the men to the lady and the lady to the men. Then the lady goes forward with a double on the left foot, and the men with theirs opposite to hers. Then the lady does another with her right foot, then the men do another, and then all of them turn round together on the right and they do two *riprese*, then they do two *continenze* together and a *reverenza* on the left foot, one facing the other, that is, the lady and the men. Then the lady does a double with her left facing the men and the men facing her; and the lady does the other with her right and the men do likewise, and at the end of their double the men turn round on the right and take the lady in the middle with a *reverenza*, and the lady does it to them: then the lady does a *movimento* and the men answer in the same manner: and begin again.

PRIMA FIGLIA GUGLIELMINO Two men and two ladies in couples, one behind the other. In this order they do two tempi of *quaternaria* doubles together, and three *contrapassi* on the left foot, ending the third with a *reverenza* in one tempo: all this is done twice. Then the men leave their lady, each one circling round his own and passing in front of her, and starting on the left foot doing two simples and four doubles, arriving at the end of these steps, in each other's place: then each man takes the lady of his companion and together they go forward with two simples and one double, starting on the left foot. Then they immediately change foot and with their left foot they do a double, the men going forward, and the ladies going backward, and with the right foot they return each to their own place from whence they started, with a double on the left. Then the men do a *meza volta* on the left. The lady in front does a *movimento*, the lady behind answers it. The man in front and the man behind set off with a double: the man in front beginning with the right foot and coming to the place of him who is behind, turning to the right and beating the ground with his left foot at the end of the tempo: the other man begins with his left foot and does the aforesaid double to the lady who was next to him, beating the ground with his right foot at the end of the tempo, turning his face to the lady who is in front. At that, the lady, the men having come round her, sets off and flees with three tempi of *piva*, and goes besides her companion on her left hand, and as she goes, the men close in next to each other with three *riprese*. Then the lady who is at the right hand of her who has just fled, passes in front of her with a double on the left foot, and he who was first her partner passes behind him who is by his side with a double on the right, and then both simultaneously beat on the *movimento*. Then the man behind and the lady who has just moved, change places with each other in three tempi of *piva*: and so it ends.

BE FIGLIA GUILIELMIN are two dances in the same canto, differently danced. The first way has already been described. The second is in the following manner. Two men and two ladies in formation, that is partners side by side together; all together they do a double with their left foot, and two fast *continenza* which they have no tempo to complete, and then they make a correct one with the right foot: then they go forward with a double, and the ladies move back with another both starting on the left foot, and they turn around and come back with a double on the right, and at the end the men turn around, but not the ladies. This is repeated twice. Then the men take the ladies by the hand and make two simples, changing places with one another and a *reverenza* each facing the other. Then they make two simples all together starting on the left foot and two doubles, and they turn around with a *ripresa* to the left, turning right round on that one step. Then another *meza volta* in *ripresa* to the right, and two doubles starting on the left, and turning around at the end with a *reverenza*, the ladies facing the men and the men facing the ladies. Then the ladies go forward towards the men with a double on the left foot, and the men do another towards them: then the ladies make another on the left and the men do a simple on the right foot and the ladies another. Then the men make a *volta tonda* starting on the right foot, and the ladies make another starting on the right foot. Then the men do a little jump and in two tempi of *piva* go towards the ladies, and the ladies go towards the men. Then the ladies make a *movimento* towards the men, and together, one behind the other, they all make slow *volte tonde* in tempo of *piva*: and then begin again.

SOBRIA as has been said before is a dance quite contrary to the MERCANTIA, in which the lady belongs only to him who first led her into the *ballo*, and it is done in six, five men and one lady, the men in pairs two by two in line, and the lady is in front hand in hand with a man. In this order they do a *saltarello* and then stop. Then the four men behind spread out with four *riprese* to form a square. Then the man in front takes the lady's hand and they both go turning around about making one *volta tonda* in *piva*, and as the man finishes the turn he lets the lady go; and she continues in *piva* and goes to the middle of the square and then stops, turning towards her partner. Then the two men in front make a double starting on the right foot and a *reverenza* holding out their hand to the lady as if to touch hers, but she refuses them her hand and timidly draws back from them, and immediately the three of them turn their backs on each other, and the men make a jump and return to their places with the same double as before; and while the men are doing their doubles the lady makes a turn. The same is repeated by the men below with the lady responding in the same way. Then the man in front turns around and comes towards the lady with two simples and a double and she goes towards him with similar steps, starting on the left foot, and he touches her hand without taking it and they both return to their places with two doubles starting on the right foot so that they have their backs to each other: then the two men in front do three tempi of *saltarello* in *quadernaria* passing into each other's place, and they come up and stand behind the lady's back, and he at the right-hand side signals to his companion to tempt the lady, and the companion signals to him to do likewise, at which the lady turns round crossly as though angered, and they with her, and with a jump they return with a double into one another's place. All this is repeated by the two men who are below, and the lady responds in the same way. Then they do a fast tempo of *saltarello*

and go to the man in front and to the lady, the men behind circling round the lady and the men in front circling round the man, and they both come together to meet each other in the middle and touch hands, then without losing a tempo the man returns to his place with two more tempi, and in her place, the lady does a *volta tonda*. Then all together the four men make three tempi of *piva* changing places one with the other, and also one simple as they arrive in each other's place. Meanwhile the man in front does a *volta tonda* in *piva*, and then the two men in front without further delay go, also in *piva*, to the place of the men behind, and the men behind go to the place of the men in front. And while they are all doing this, the lady in her turn also does a *volta tonda* in *piva*, and her partner goes to fetch her in *piva* and leads her out in *piva*, while the four men below close in together in *riprese*, reforming themselves into couples side by side, and so begin again.

These said dances are all the grand and pre-eminent *balli* recently created by the King of that art, my only master and compatriot MisserDomenichino of Piacenza, honoured cavalier renowned for his perfect and famous craft.

There are endless other *balli* and *bassedanze*, which because they are either too old or too well known, I will pass by in silence, as for instance, L'INGRATA, LA PIZOCHARA, PRECIGOGNA, FIDEL RITORNO, EL ZOIOSO, LEONCELLO FOR TWO, BERREGUARDO FOR TWO, ANELLO, GELLOSIA, PRESONIERA, MADAMA GENEVRA, MARCHESANA, BEL FIORE, LA SEVE, LEVORETTA, BASSADANZA SECRETA, LA REALE, FODRA and THE OLD MIGNOTTA, etc. with many others.

I will now describe the new *Bassadanza* which are more beautiful than the others, and I will then mark the procedures which are best and more esteemed by their excellence in refined assembly rooms by good dancers.

MIGNOTTA NOVA is danced by a man and a lady in single file, and as many others as wish to dance provided the room is large and spacious. They begin with two *continenze*, and with the left foot they do two simples and one double, and come back on the right foot taking a little step backwards and sideways, and then another on the left foot still diagonally. Then they go forward with a double on the right foot and then *two continenze*. Then two doubles starting on the left foot and two more *continenze*. Then diagonally they do a *ripresa* on the left. Then they come back starting on the right foot, and a double and a simple in one tempo, then another double, and they do a little step diagonally on the left, and another still diagonally on the right. And at this point he who was last now becomes first. Then, as at the beginning, they go forward with a double on the left and a diagonal *ripresa* on the right. Then two *continenze* and then they begin two slow tempo of *saltarello* in *bassadanza* and then a double on the left foot. Then two simples, starting on the right foot. Then three *contrapassi* on the right foot, within two of *bassadanza*, and a *reverenza* on the left, and so begin again.

DAMNES is a *bassadanza* that is danced in three, two men and one lady, with the lady in the middle. Together they do two *continenze*. Then the men change places with each other doing two simples in this manner; they do a *ripresa* as they turn around from the simples, and then go back to their own places with the same steps starting on the right foot. Meanwhile the lady does a *volta tonda*, and all together they then do a *ripresa* on the right, and a *reverenza* on the left. Then the lady does two simples and four doubles around the men in this way, beginning with her left foot and returning to her place; but, as she is completing her two tempi, the man in front circles round her with doubles and goes to his place, and the other man behind then does likewise, and when she has returned to her place they do two *riprese* all together and a *reverenza* on the left. Then the lady sets off from the men and the men from the lady all at once: she goes forward with two simples and two doubles, and she turns around in two *riprese*, and the men do a *ripresa* backwards on the left side, and another on the right side, and one more *ripresa* to the left and a *volta tonda*. Then the men go towards the lady with two simples and two doubles and the lady does a circle in the same steps, and when they have all finished, the lady is found to be in the middle, and they do two *riprese*, then two *continenze*. Then they all turn facing the same way and do four tempi of *saltarello* in single file.

Then they all do a *ripresa* and come back with two simples and one double. They then do two more simples and one double the opposite way (they turn about) then a *volta tonda* and a *reverenza*: and so it ends.

CORONA *bassadanza* is danced like the Mignotta in single file. Two simples beginning on the left foot, with two doubles on the right foot. Followed by a double with the left foot. Followed by one *cambiamento* starting with the right foot, a double on the left foot and a simple on the right foot which then completes the tempo. Then one does a *meza volta* turning to the left with a simple step on the left foot in the void, jumping on to the right foot and turning round with a double on the right foot, doing a *meza volta* on that same foot with two *riprese* one on the left and the other on the right. Followed by a *cambiamento* starting with the left foot with two doubles on the right foot, making a *mezavolta* on the right foot and doing a double on the left foot with another on the right. Afterwards a *cambiamento* starting with the left foot and then leaping on to the right foot with *mezavolta* turning to the right, making four movements of *quaternaria* in the *bassadanza* measure, making a *volta tonda* round to the right with a diagonal *ripresa* with the left foot, turning round with a *meza volta* over to the left, with a diagonal *ripresa* with the right foot and turning round. Afterwards two *continenze* with two *riprese* one on the left and the other on the right, jumping on to the left foot in the void, with a double on the right foot and with a *ripresa* diagonally forward on the left foot. Then a simple step in the void with the right foot, leaping on to that one, and doing a *ripresa* on to the left side diagonally forward. Afterwards a *volta tonda* with a *reverenza*; and it is finished: but this is the very greatest *bassadanza*, not for people who blot their copy book, and as has been said, the very crown of all the others.

Now we come to the tenor for the *bassadanza* and the *saltarelli*, the ones which are best and more often used than all the others.
There are many other tenors for the *saltarelli* and *bassadanza*,

but these are the most frequently used. It should be noted that every tenor can be done in four measures, and to a good musician the first is its own natural measure which divides the beat by three, and this is danced as *saltarello* by us Italians.

Second in *quaternaria*, dividing the beat by four, and in dancing, this is more often used by the Germans.

Third the chase, is a measure known as *piva*, some call it the child of the *quaternaria* because to every note there are many beats; but they are faster in the execution.

Fourth is the *Bassadanza*, the imperial measure where each note is redoubled, and the three are worth six, and the six twelve. But in dancing all these measures one finds variations in their tempi other than breadth, as is apparent above.

The measure of the *bassadanza* begins with the void and ends with the full. The measure of the *quaternaria* begins with the full and has the void in the middle and also at the end.

The *saltarello* follows the style of the *bassadanza* in this.

The *piva* follows the style of the *quaternaria*.

That which is the void and that which is the full, I should have explained to Your Grace Illus. S. Sforza, but these are things which are not to be explained with words; but I am certain that if Your Grace turns your attention and ingenuity to it, and you get your musicians to play you these measures, you will come to understand it better than I could ever explain it, and so I excuse myself from this burden.

FINIS

Notes

INTRODUCTION

1. Translated into English by Sir Thomas Hoby in 1561.
2. Translated into English by Edward Dacres in 1640.
3. Edited by J. Meyer—Library of National Antiquities.
4. 'Beatrice d'Este Duchess of Milan', Julia Cartwright 1899.
5. 'Le Lettere di Messer Andrea Calmo', Vittorio Rossi, Turin 1888.
6. 'Ledivico Novello Mascharate', pub. 1546.
7. Published by Dance Horizons Inc., New York.
8. 'Isabella d'Este Marchioness of Mantua', Julia Cartwright 1903.
9. 'The Memoirs of Philip de Commines', ed. A. R. Scoble 1856.

THE ART OF DANCING

Page 18, line 2 *Misura*. It is very difficult to find an English word which covers exactly what Cornazano seems to mean by *misura*, we have therefore used the literal translation of 'measure'.

In the opening paragraph Cornazano suggests that measure means keeping in time with and responding to the music. In other places he uses the word to indicate the different musical proportions or to refer to the rhythm of the music. Certainly he always uses the term in a musical context and not, as in sixteenth-century England, where measure was used simply as another word for 'dance'.

Page 18, line 8: It is interesting to note that Cornazano uses the singular which suggests that he expects the dances to be accompanied by one musician rather than by a consort, and in the work of Cornazano's contemporary Guglielmo Ebreo there is a miniature of three dancers being accompanied by a single harp.

Page 18, line 10: *Campeggiando et ondeggiando*. These two words set a problem. *Ondeggiando* means 'undulating' and Cornazano later explains that this applies to the soft rise and fall of the feet making the steps. *Campeggiare* according to an Italian/English dictionary dated 1611 *Queen Anna's new world of words* means:

to encamp, to beleagre, or lie in the field with an army of men. Also to dwell among or frequent the fields. Also to sute or square with, to become well and seemly as any faine cock upon or in any field, shield or banner.

C. Mazzi in an article on Cornazano's manuscript in *La Bibliofilia* (1915) suggests that the word means a sideways undulation as opposed to an up and down one, but nothing in the translation of the word seems to bear this out.

Otto Kinkeldey in *A Jewish Dancing Master of the Renaissance* (1929) translates the word as 'to posture to pose or to balance', which comes a little nearer the original 'to encamp'.

Whenever Cornazano uses the word he seems to be implying that the foot upon which one must *campeggiare* is placed firmly on the floor and carries the weight of the body while the other foot moves:

> ... so that if you move the right foot to make a double you must *campeggiare* (balance) on the left foot which remains firm on the ground.

We have therefore used the word 'balance' to translate *campeggiare* throughout the text.

Page 18, line 22: *Sempii* (mod. It. *Scempii* meaning single). English sixteenth-century dance manuscripts call these steps 'singles' while Thoinot Arbeau in his *Orchesographie* (1589) calls them 'simples'.

Page 18, line 22: *Dopii* (meaning 'doubles'). These steps are called doubles both by Arbeau and in the English manuscripts, presumably because each one is double the length of a simple in note value.

Page 18, line 22: *Riprese* (mod. It. *Ripresa* meaning 'recovery' or 'resumption'). Burgundian *basses danses* of the 15th century include a step called a *demarche* which Arbeau calls a *reprise*, and both of these appear to involve a movement backwards. Caesare Negri in *Il Gratie d'Amore* (1602) describes a *Ripresa Grave* which is done by:

> moving the left foot to the side ... and after lifting somewhat both heels then drawing the right to the left you have to lower them both together.

Page 18, line 22: *Continente* (meaning 'restrained' or 'temperate').
This step is not used in the Burgundian manuscripts although certain Spanish manuscripts of the fifteenth century use the name for the step called *Branle* in the Burgundian dances. Fabritio Caroso in *Il Ballarino* (1581) and Caesare Negri in *Il Gratie d'Amore* (1602) describe this step as follows:

> move to the left side four fingers breadths drawing the heel of the right foot towards the middle of the left (foot) and in making which bend slightly with the body and rise as gracefully as possible ... and peacocking a little towards the side to which it is made.

Page 18, line 22: *Volte Tonde* (meaning 'full turns'). Cornazano suggests later in the work that in the *Bassa danza* this full turn must be done with specific steps (see note page 27, line 32).

Page 18, line 22: *Mezo Volte* (meaning 'half turn').

Page 19, line 6: My Lady Beatrice—this was Beatrice d'Este, sister of Duke Borso of Ferrara, and at the time of this manuscript married to Borso di Gherardo da Correggio, and living in Ferrara. She later married Tristan Sforza and spent the rest of her life in Milan where Hyppolita may perhaps have met her on visits to her native town.

Page 19, line 10: Piero Bono—a celebrated lutenist of the period attached to the court of Ferrara.

Page 19, line 12: Duke Borso—Borso d'Este, first Duke of Ferrara (1430–1471). This proverb in praise of the d'Este family suggests that Cornazano was, or had been, employed by them and worked at Ferrara.

Page 19, line 15: *Piva* (mod. It. meaning bagpipes). As Cornazano explains later this name is derived from the rustic origins of this particular dance rhythm, being, he says, the music played by shepherd's on their reed pipes.

Page 19, line 15: *Saltarello* (from *saltare* 'to jump, skip, spring). *Queen Anna's New World of Words* gives *Saltarello* as 'any little leape'

Page 19, line 16: *Quaternaria* (no modern equivalent). Literally means a unit of four.

Page 19, line 16: *Bassadanza*. This corresponds to the *Basses Danses* of the fifteenth-century Burgundian manuscripts, in one of which it is described as being so called:

> because when one dances it one goes naturally without stirring oneself as graciously as one might

while another says:

> because when one dances it one goes in peace without stirring oneself as graciously as one might

Mabel Dolmetch in *Dances of France and England* takes this to mean that it is a slow stately dance with no energetic movements. Melusine Wood, however, in *Some Historical Dances* interprets it as meaning that it is a country dance which should not be too stately. Cornazano describes it as 'the queen of measures' which suggests that it is indeed graceful and stately, but at the same time, both he and his contemporaries include *saltarello* (any little leape) in their *basse danze*.

Page 19, line 19: *Alta Danza*. Cornazano defines this as the name given by the Spaniards to *Saltarello* or *Pas de Brebant*. The Burgundian manuscripts describe the *Pas de Brebant* as the *Basse danse mineur*, which was always danced before the *Basse danse* proper. Many of the Italian *balli* also begin with several tempi of *Saltarello* before the rhythm changes to *Bassa danza*.

Page 19, line 22: *Tempo*. Here again it is difficult to translate this word exactly. Cornazano does not use the word in quite the same sense as it is used today to indicate the speed of the music. He sometimes uses it to refer to the beat or pulse of the music, but at other times he could be referring to bars of music (see note page 22, line 17), while on other occasions he means quite literally 'time', e.g. eleven tempi (times) of *saltarello*.

Page 20, line 14: See note for page 21, line 5.

Page 20, line 16: *La donna deve mai dispiccare el suo tempo da terra*. Queen Anna's *New World of Words* gives *dispiccare* as 'to unhang' while *spiccare* means 'to plucke from or off, to unfasten or separate from. Also to skip or leape off'. This seems to imply that the lady should not jump. However as the step is called *saltarello* meaning 'any little leape' and as Cornazano goes on to say that the man should not do it either, this would not make much sense. It is possible that he means she should only jump if she is doing the 'natural' *Saltarello*, but not if she is doing variations on it. Another possible interpretation is that he is trying to tell his reader she must not jump so high that she gets out of time with the music, in other words, when she jumps she must land on the beat of the music.

Page 20, line 29: See note for page 19, line 22.

Page 21, line 5: *Contrapassi* (meaning countersteps, or cross steps). In the light of Cornazano's suggestion that the lady may make 3 *contrapassi* in 2 beats, this would appear to mean steps going across the rhythm, similar perhaps to the hemiolas in Galliards. Indeed one often finds that where Cornazano says 3 *contrapassi*, Domenico will say 2 doubles.

Page 21, line 5: *Movimenti* (meaning 'movements' or 'stirrings').

Page 21, line 6: *Scambii* (meaning exchanges).

Page 21, line 6: *Trascorse* (meaning overrunnings or passings).

Page 21, line 6: *Frappamenti* (meaning beatings).

Page 21, line 7: *Pizigamenti* (meaning pinchings, pluckings or dodgings).

Page 21, line 17: *Saltarello Todescho* (meaning literally German little leaps). Cornazano says that this step is also called *Quaternaria* and later defines *Quaternaria* as 'dividing the beat by four', i.e. duple time. Thoinot Arbeau in his Orchesographie describes a dance called *Allemande* (meaning German) and several sixteenth-century English manuscripts include dances called Almaines. The one characteristic of all these sixteenth-century dances is a double step with a hop at the end danced in duple time.

Page 21, line 33: *Ballitti*—*Ballo* is a dance, *ballitto* a little dance.

Page 22, line 12: See note for page 21, line 33.

Page 22, line 14: *Dicto Facto*—literally 'said and done' or without more ado. In spite of this boast we find that Cornazano's description of certain dances does not fit easily with the music, while the same dances as described by his teacher Domenico are very easily interpreted. One must suspect therefore that Cornazano's memory was not always as good as he says.

Page 22, line 17: *Dui passi sempi sono un tempo*. In this instance I believe Cornazano is referring to a musical unit similar to that indicated in the Burgundian manuscripts written at the same time, where the following rule is given:

> It must be understood that two simple steps, one double step, one *demarche* and one *branle* take up as much time as each other, that is to say that each of them must take up one complete note of *basse danse*.

One complete note of *basse danse* in modern musical terms is one bar of 6/8, so Cornazano's words could be translated 'Two simple steps equal one bar'.

Page 22, line 29: *Un misurare l'aere nel levamento dell'ondeggiare*. A rather enigmatic sentence. Cornazano is probably referring to his earlier description of *Maniera* (manner) and *Aere* (spirit), i.e. the ability to move with such grace and poise that the audience will take pleasure in watching one.

Page 23, line 9: *Havere la palma*—literally 'to carry the palm'. Those who wish to achieve the highest accolate must climb the ladder.

Page 23, line 24: The whole of this section (to page 24, line 7) can only make sense if the words *Piva, Saltarello, Quadernaria* and *Bassa Danza* refer to musical rhythms, rather than specific steps. There were certain steps which were more common to one rhythm than to another, but these steps could also be done in other rhythms though the manner of performing them would have to be varied to make them fit the music. The purpose of the ladder is also emphasised here in that the changes from one rhythm to another must be in strict proportion. Cornazano and his contemporaries used certain symbols in the music to indicate these proportions:

> O = saltarello
> ₵ = bassa danza
> C = quadernaria

In this instance therefore he is saying that, given that Piva rhythm is a fast 3/4 one can dance a typical Quaternaria or 4/4 step to two bars of Piva, but the step will have to be drawn out somewhat to fit the music, possible as follows:

> 1 2 3 1 2 3 Piva rhythm
> 1   2 3   4 Quaternaria steps

Page 25, line 15: MERCANTIA. Also described with slight differences in Manuscript 972 Bibliothèque Nationale, Paris, in a work ascribed to Domenico da Piacenza *c.* 1440, whom Cornazano refers to as 'my only master and compatriot'. It is also described in a slightly different form by two other writers of the same period, Guglielmo Ebreo and Johannis Ambrosio who also claimed to be pupils of Domenico.

Page 25, line 28: *Senza perdere tempo*—literally 'without losing a beat', in other words the turn is part of the following two simples rather than taking up any music of its own.

Page 26, line 16: JOVE. Also described by Guglielmo and by Ambrosio, and under the name of *Jupiter* by Domenico.

Page 26, line 29: *Col pie stancho*—literally 'with the tired foot'. We have assumed here that *tired* or *faint* means *left*, especially as in this particular case the left foot is free anyway. Queen Anna's New World of Words gives *Stancomano* as 'left-handed'. It is impossible to say however why Cornazano should suddenly use this term, and why only in this one dance.

Page 27, line 4: VERZEPPE. Also described by Domenico.

Page 27, line 32: In many of the basse dances described by Guglielmo and Ambrosio they specify that the *volta tonda* is done with 'two simples beginning with the right foot and a *ripresa* on the right'. Presumably this way of doing the movement was for Basse Dances only and Cornazano is here suggesting that in *Balli*, the movement can be done in other ways and can begin with the left foot.

Page 27, line 34: BEREGUARDO NOVA. Also described by Domenico and Guglielmo. Belriguardo was a villa of the d'Este family 12 miles from Ferrara on the banks of the river Po. When Hyppolita's brother Lodovico Sforza visited it in 1493 he said, 'I would not for all the world have missed seeing this place. Really I do not think I have ever seen so large and fine a house or one so well laid out and adorned with such excellent pictures' (*Beatrice d'Este Duchess of Milan* by Julia Cartwright).

Page 28, line 7: *Reverentia* (mod. It. *Riverenza* meaning 'curtesey', 'reverence'). Reverence is the standard term for bows and curtseys used by dancing masters throughout Europe from the fifteenth to the eighteenth century.

Page 28, line 31: LEONCELLO NOVA. Also described by Domenico.

Page 29, line 21: PRIMA FIGLIA GUGLIELMIN. Also described by Domenico and Guglielmo.

Page 31, line 3: SOBRIA. Also described by Domenico.

Page 32, line 22: Some of the dances described by Cornazano as 'too old or too well known' appear in the other dance treatise as follows:

	Domenico	*Ambrosio*	*Guglielmo*
Ingrata	*	*	*
Pizochara	*	*	*
Zioiosa (Gioiosa)		*	*
Leoncello (for 2)	*	*	*
Berreguardo (for 2)	*	*	*
Anello	*	*	*
Gellosia	*	*	*
Presoniera		*	*
Genevra (Bassa Danza)		*	*
Marchesana	*	*	*
Bel fiore	*	*	*
Reale (Bassa Danza)		*	*
Mignotta (Bassa Danza)	*	*	*

As Domenico was the teacher of the other three, it is generally assumed that his treatise was the first to be written. Cornazano's treatise is dated 1455 and one of the Guglielmo manuscripts is dated 1463. This suggests that Domenico's own work was written *c*. 1440. Some of the dances described by Cornazano as 'too old or too well known' are included in both Domenico and Guglielmo which suggests that they survived in popularity for at least 20 years. It is interesting to note that there are references to three of Guglielmo's dances in the letters of Andrea Calmo, and in a song text published 1546 (see Introduction, p. 11) which indicates that the dances remained popular for a great many years. We know that the Burgundian *basses danses* survived for nearly 100 years.

Page 34, line 14: *Cambiamento*. The same as *scambii*.

Page 34, line 28: *Una ripresa sul gallone*. C. Mazzi can find no explanation for this phrase since the word *gallone* in modern Italian means 'braid, or gallon measure' and he suggests that it is a misprint for *tallone* meaning heel. The word does appear however in *Queen Anna's New World of Words* as 'a Man's thigh, hip or hanch', and it is probable therefore that Cornazano is suggesting a sideways or diagonal movement.

Page 35, line 20: The work is dedicated to Hippolyta Sforza, Duchess of Calabria (see Introduction, pp. 13–14).

Music for
The Book on
The Art of Dancing

Transcribed by Mary Criswick

MUSIC

Cornazano gives the music for the seven *balli* described by him, and also three *tenore* which he says are 'the best and most often used' to accompany the *bassa danza* or *saltarello*. Since the three pieces of music do not have the same titles as any of the *basse danze* he describes, it would seem that the dance musician could take any well-known *tenore* and adapt it to fit the particular dance the dancers wanted to perform.

A *tenore* was used as a basic note pattern which provided a ground around which the other instruments would weave their own independent melody, and as we have seen, one bar of music equals one double or two simple steps (see note 29).

In the case of the *balli* these are marked *in canto* meaning 'in song notation'. They should not, however, be taken as melodies. In spite of the different notation they are still a very skeletal note pattern and should be treated in the same way as the *bassa danza tenore*.

Mercantia in canto

Giove in canto

Verzeppe in canto

Bereguardo in canto

Leoncello in canto (*to be danced twice*)

Filia Guilielmino in canto (*to be danced twice*)

Sobria in canto

Tenore del Re di Spagna

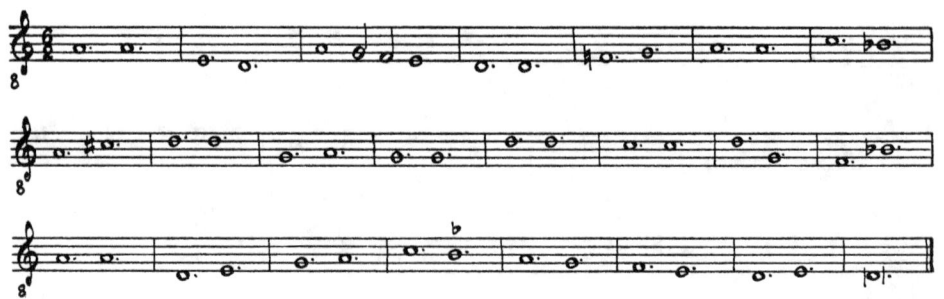

Canzon de pifari dico el Ferrarese

Tenore Collinetto